Danny, the Duck with no QUACK

Malachy Doyle
Janet Samuel

QEB Publishing

Every morning, the ducks and the hens gather in the yard for a chat.

"How's the quack, Danny?" asks a chicken. "What's the story? Tell us the news."

But Danny's a shy little duck,
and he never knows what to say.

He keeps his beak
firmly shut, bows his
head, and turns away.

"Come on, Danny!" squawk the birds one day. "Don't be such a scaredy-quack! There must be something you can tell us!"

Danny swallows and opens his beak—but nothing comes out.

Not a peep, not a splutter, not a cackle, not a hoot. He's **lost his quack!**

Right, thinks Danny, that's it.
And he takes off up the lane
to find a tale worth telling.

Yes, he wanders up the track
to find his quack.

He waddles along and waddles along,
till he meets two scrawny foxes.

This thing's heavy!

Who'll help us carry it?

That duck!

"We've carried it far enough," groans one fox. "Now who'll collect the wood?"

"The duck with no quack," sniffs the other.

And Danny knows he shouldn't
—these are hungry-looking foxes.
He opens his mouth to say no.

But he can't.

"Now who'll fill the pot with water?"
asks one fox.
"The duck with no quack,"
smirks the other.

And Danny knows he shouldn't
—these are scary-looking foxes.

He opens his beak as wide as he
can, and what does he say?

Nothing.

"Now who'll be the dinner?"
says one fox, licking his lips.

"The duck with no quack!' cries the other, jumping up.

They rush toward Danny and they're just about to grab him, when...

"Quackity-quack! It's a duck attack!" squawks Danny.

He throws himself to the side
of the pot.

The two foxes are so surprised,
they tumble right inside!

"How's the quack, Danny?" ask the other ducks,
when he rushes back to the farmyard.
"Yeah, what's the cluck, duck?" ask the hens.

And aren't they all
amazed to hear
Danny quacking?

Aren't they all
astonished at the
tale he has to tell?

"I wandered down the track and I met a pair of foxes..."

"They were carrying a pot, and I knew they wanted to cook me..."

"They made me gather wood..."

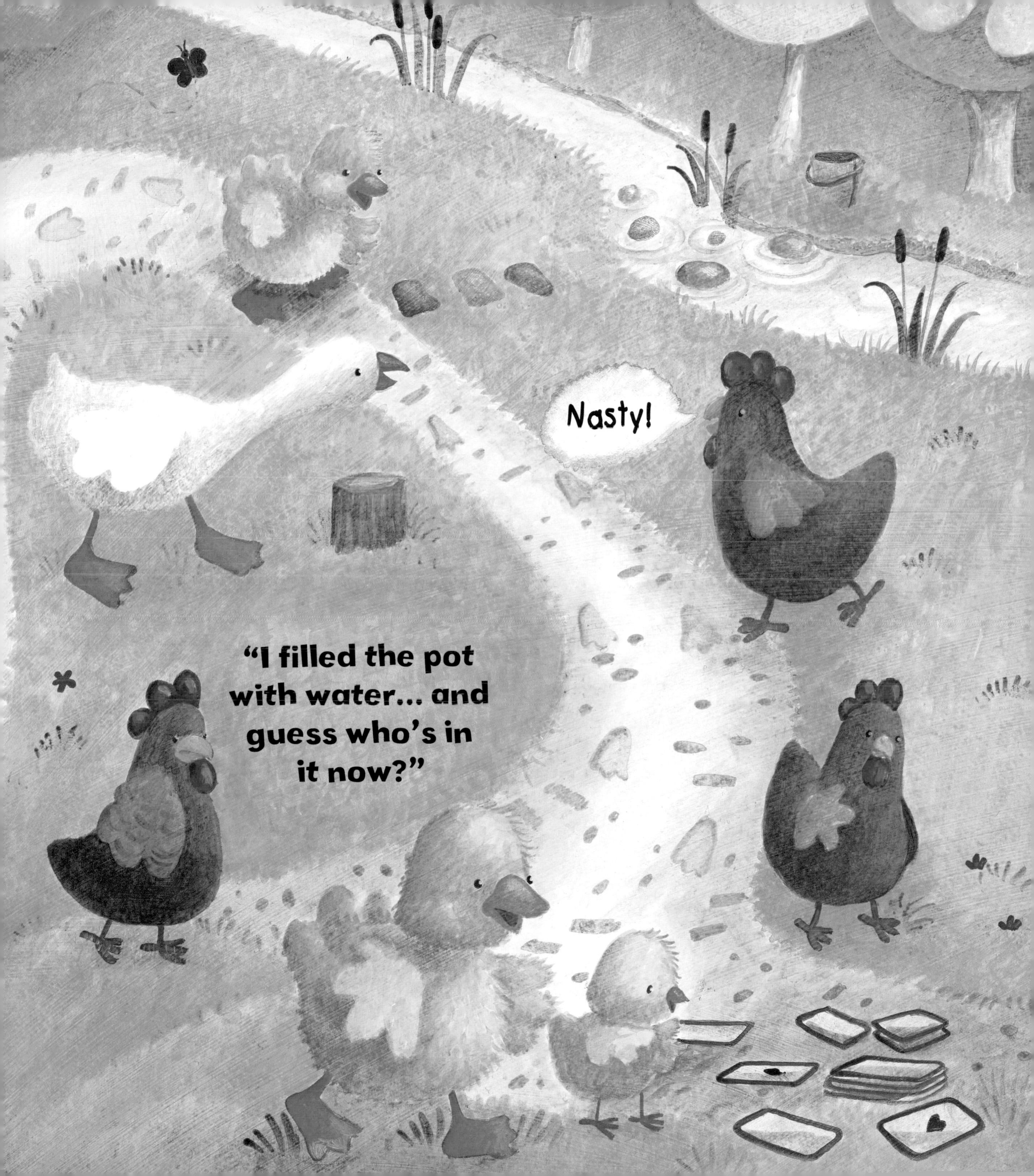

"I filled the pot with water... and guess who's in it now?"

"Go away!" cluck the angry hens.

"And don't come back!" quack the ducks.

And Danny's quack is the loudest.

"Quackity-quack!" he says. "Don't come back!"

Notes for parents and teachers

- After you have read this book with a child or children, there are many ways you can extend their interest in and enjoyment of the story.

- At the start of the story, the ducks and hens have a chat. Ask the children what they would talk about. Then ask them to chat together as though they are the birds.

- Ask the children to act out the whole story. One is Danny, two are the foxes, and the others are the farmyard birds and animals. Ask them to move and talk like the characters would move and talk. Then ask the children how they feel.

- Danny is a shy little duck. Ask the children if they know anyone who they think is shy and what it would feel like. Can they think of a time when they felt particularly shy? When was it and what happened?

- Ask the children to pretend to be Danny and tell the story from his point of view. For example, "I'm a shy little duck and I often don't know what to say...". Then they can pretend to be one of the foxes and tell the story from his point of view. For example, "One day I was in the wood with my friend and I found a pot...".

- Help the children to make hand puppets of Danny and the two foxes out of paper bags, old gloves, or old socks. They can then use the puppets to re-enact the story.

- With the children, make a map of Danny's journey. Draw, or write, what happened along the way. Ask the children to point to where each event took place as you re-tell the story.

- Ask the children to list the four things the foxes asked Danny to do. How many did he do, and why didn't he do the last one?

- When the foxes ask Danny to carry the pot, he knows he should say no but he can't find the words. Have any of the children ever wanted to say no but were not able to? What did they wish they had said or done?

- Do the children think Danny had changed by the end of the story? How and why has he changed?

- Did anyone feel sorry for the foxes ending up in the pot? Do they think the ducks and hens should have left them there? Why do they think the ducks and hens let them out?

Copyright © QEB Publishing, Inc. 2009

Published in the United States by
QEB Publishing, Inc.
3 Wrigley, Suite A
Irvine, CA 92618
www.qeb-publishing.com

A CIP record for this book is available from the Library of Congress.

ISBN 978-1-59566-873-8

Printed and bound in China

Author Malachy Doyle
Illustrator Janet Samuel
Designer Alix Wood
Project Editor Heather Amery

Publisher Steve Evans
Creative Director Zeta Davies
Managing Editor Amanda Askew